Piero Torriti

Superintendent of the Artistic and
Historical Assets for the Provinces
of Siena and Gr...

A DAY IN

SAN GIMIGNANO

THE TOWN OF THE FAIR TOWERS

126 COLOUR ILLUSTRATIONS
MAP OF THE TOWN

BET

BONECHI EDIZIONI "IL TURISMO" FIRENZE

INDEX

View of San Gimignano.

HISTORICAL NOTES

The first settlement to rise upon the hill of today's San Gimignano, was almost undoubtedly Etruscan. A number of archaeological finds and tombs have been brought to light, but the local dialect and even the place-names of the district evoke their Etruscan origin, see for instance: Capassi (from "cape" or "aska"=containers), Cellole (from Cel=sun and mother of Celsclan or Cela=cell?).

After the power of the Etruscans fell, a Roman fort was erected on this hill, that was to take the name of Silvia, or Castle of the Selva (Wood). The thick, wide-spread forests that covered the area must have inspired the many names based on tree-species, such as Via Quercecchio (oak?), Via del Prunello (prunus?), etc. It was only after the advent of Christianity, that the burg took the name of St. Gimignano, Bishop of Modena (who died in 387), who, according to legend, saved the citizens of the little town from the onslaughts of the Barbarian hordes. Another legend reports that Desiderius, king of the Longobards resided in what is today known as the tower of the Pesciolini; the legend continues asserting that Charlemagne

3

also sojourned there. On the other hand, the names of Cortennano, Pancole, Caggio, Via Bonda (boundary) certainly indicate a Longobard heritage, as do certain terms used in old matrimonial contracts (antefato) stored in the old city archives, in the descriptions of dowries (guadia) and in the actual stipulation of the marriages (mogliazzi). The first written record of San Gimignano, however appeared in 929, when the Marquis Hugo of Tuscany made gift of its lands to Abelard, Bishop of Volterra, which diocese San Gimignano belonged to until 1782, when it was assigned to the diocese of Colle Val d'Elsa. The Bishop of Volterra had his Castle-Fortress in San Gimignano as well (see p. 65). The first circle of the walls, which included the still visible Arch (city gate) of the Becci and Cugnanesi and the Cancelleria (Chancellory) Arch, was built some time around the 12th century and surrounded the hill known as Montestaffoli (mount of Astolphus, the Longobard prince?) and was about 1100 metres long. It was within these walls that the lords of the surrounding countryside built their tower houses, so as to protect themselves from the periodic invasions that swept through the land. The second circle of walls, built around the 14th century, was built to shelter the increased population. The authority of the Commune started to override the Bishop's and between the 14th and 15th centuries, San Gimignano found itself full of hostels, tower palaces, churches and monasteries. The dominant faction was the Guelph one and it was to this Guelph audience that the Florentine ambassador, Dante Alighieri addressed his famous speech in the great council hall of the Commune on the 8th May 1300 (see p. 48). San Gimignano chiefly owes its impressive, flourishing growth to the great road that drove through it from gate to gate: the Via Francigena or Via Romea, that the Longobards had strengthened against the Byzantines in order to ensure a safe thoroughfare for their people on their way down through the Alps to the South of Italy — a branch of it was then to lead to Rome (which would be most trod upon during the Holy Years, one of the most famous of which was 1300). The road traversed San Gimignano and taverns, rest-houses, hostels and the great Mansions of the Knights Templar or the Knights of Malta sprung up on either side of it. Trade grew with them, bringing wealth if not peace, for the citizens of San Gimignano were ever a restless and quarrelsome people.

Decadence first set in when the area and the city of Siena were conquered by the Spanish troops of Charles Vth and by Cosimo Ist's Medici militia in 1555. The latter, by then Lord of all Tuscany, even issued a decree forbidding any monies spent on either religious or civilian buildings which might lead to the enlargement of the little town of San Gimignano (1563). This decree naturally gave rise to much suffering and poverty, but was also the salvation of the ancient houses, towers, and medieval churches, as they were thus prevented from being knocked down and subjected to Baroque restructuring, preserved to this day in the original state to which San Gimignano of the beautiful towers owes its fame.

FIRST ITINERARY

Cathedral Square — Collegiata Cathedral — Piazza Pecori — Museum of Religious Art — Archaeological Museum — Palace of the Commune — Civic Museum

The Cathedral square from the steps of the Cathedral.

PIAZZA DEL DUOMO

The heart of the town is the Cathedral Square, where the three most important medieval buildings in the town face each other across its stone flags: the *Cathedral of the Collegiata*, the old *Palace of the Podestà* and the *Palace of the Commune* (or *New Palace of the Podestà*). The elder of the two latter buildings

5

Two views of the Palace of the Podestà and the "Rognosa"
(Scurvy) Tower.

faces the Cathedral from the opposite side of the square. It
used to be the residence of the Podestà and his family and it
was the seat of the Council. It is one of the oldest structures in
town, surmounted by its 13th century tower known as the
"Rognosa" (Scurvy), which is 51 meters high. The Statutes of
1255 established that no other tower should be higher than the
tower of the palace of the Podestà, the only exception being
the Torre Grossa (Great Tower) of the Palace of the Commune
which is 53 metres high.

On the ground floor of the Palace of the Podestà, there is a
kind of great porch covered by a spacious vaulted ceiling and
surrounded by stone wall-benches. On the end wall: the
dilapidated traces of a fresco painted by Sodoma in 1513,
showing the *Madonna and Child between Saints Nicholas and
Gimignano*. Inside, the palace was restructured in 1534 with a
view to building a theatre within the palace, that was to be
totally retransformed in 1794 by Francesco Marinelli and is
today completely abandoned. The battlements at the top of the
façade are also a recent addition.

Palazzo Paltoni-Salvucci, with its twin towers is to the left of
the Cathedral steps, if one is facing downhill. On the other side
of the street, to the right of the Palace of the Podestà (to the left
of the onlooker on the steps of the Cathedral), see the elegant
Palazzo Useppi-Chigi, with its late 13th century tower.

Left: **the eastern side of the Cathedral square;** *right:* **the Paltoni-Salvucci Palace, with its twin towers.**

The Palace of the Commune is to ones right, but we shall describe it after visiting the Cathedral of the Collegiata.

THE COLLEGIATA CATHEDRAL

This majestic religious edifice, which is, as we shall see, chiefly renowned for the extraordinarily interesting cycles of frescoes all over its inner walls, was built in the 12th century and, according to tradition, consecrated in 1148 by Pope Eugene III. The little apse, pertaining to a small Protoromanesque church, which has recently come to light within the church, next to the façade of the existing church seems to prove that the latter was built on the same site as the earlier structure, the chief difference being that the original church faced uphill instead of downhill, as the Collegiata does.

FAÇADE. — The existing façade of the cathedral, however, only came into existence in 1239, when Master Matteo Bruni - send built the two side-doors without planning a central one, with the probable intention of respecting the apse of the earlier church we have just mentioned. The façade was unfortunately subjected to heavy restructuring and was even

The façade of the Cathedral of the Collegiata.

covered with stucco decoration and painted with a series of squares by one Tommaso Baldini in 1818. In 1896 it was restored to its present state. The two doors were originally slightly narrower and were enlarged when the church was restructured between the 14th and 15th centuries.

INTERIOR. — The Collegiata contains inestimable art-treasures. Fundamentally, the interior is still essentially Romanesque in character. The three aisles are defined by a series of arches, that divide the length of the main body of the church into seven spans, supported by solid stone columns crowned by fine Romanesque capitals.

A monochrome *frieze* by Pier Francesco Fiorentino (1474), showing *cherubs* holding garlands below the figures of ten *apostles* and two other *figures*, decorates the walls facing into the central nave.

Above: interior of the Collegiata; *below*: Madonna and Child
with two saints, by Memmo di Filippuccio.

Martyrdom of St. Sebastian, by Benozzo Gozzoli.

CENTRAL NAVE. — A fine wooden *pulpit* is supported by the fourth column on the right. The inlaid panels are by Antonio da Colle (1469). At the end of the central nave there is a *Christ laid out at the sepulchre* by Sebastiano Mainardi on the triumphal arch.

The first span of the central nave vaulting is frescoed with the *Four Evangelists* by Taddeo di Bartolo, while the intrados' of

Angel and Virgin Annunciate, by Jacopo della Quercia.

the arches are decorated with the figures of *Prophets, Saints* and *Virtues* by Taddeo di Bartolo and Benozzo Gozzoli.

INNER FAÇADE. — Above the doorways, there are still visible traces of the earliest frescoes painted in the Collegiata which are to be considered more or less contemporary to the traces of a gigantic *St. Christopher* underlying the Bartolo di Fredi frescoes and can almost certainly be identified as the frescoes painted by Memmo di Filippuccio, father of Lippo and Federico Memmi, in 1305. Memmo's scenes are arranged on three levels, starting with the *Miracle of St. Nicholas of Bari* in which the saint gives the three unmarried spinsters three bags of gold as their dowry. This scene is followed by another one, less easy to identify. Above the door is a *Madonna and Child*, with *two Saints* and *two adoring angels.* Further traces of frescoes in the upper register show two *dead or sleeping women* as well as the *Martyrdom of a Saint being boiled alive in a cauldron.* Memmo's work can however be more easily appreciated in the Palace of the Commune.

The central area of the inner façade (where one can still detect the little apse of the earlier Protoromanesque church which proves that the early church faced uphill) is decorated with a series of magnificent frescoes centering around the *Martyrdom of St. Sebastian*, by Benozzo Gozzoli dated around 1465. It reminds one of an allegorical Mystery Play scene, as it is distinctly medieval in character, with the onlookers arranged in a wide circle around the central figure of the Saint that include Jesus and the Mother. The whole is framed by a series of figures of saints worked into a decorative frieze; at the bottom is a *Crucifixion flanked by Saints Jerome and Onofrio*. In front of the fresco are the two splendid painted wooden statues of the *Virgin* and the *Announcing Angel* carved some time after 1421 by Jacopo della Quercia and painted in 1426 by Martino di Bartolommeo. The signature of the sculptor is cut into the base of the Announcing Angel, while the painter's is discernible on the base of the statue of the Virgin. They are a truly admirable group, in which the great Jacopo della Quercia has tried to overcome all the Gothic tenets, employing a rigorous realism in the description of the figures, specially in the Annunciate Virgin, whose perfect balance is enhanced by the delicate grace of her half-turned body. The mediating rôle played by Jacopo between the Gothic flexuosity of Giovanni Pisano and the advanced Renaissance solidity of Michelangelo is marvellously apparent in this delicate early flowering of Renaissance ideas. The whole of the upper register of the counter-façade is covered with frescoes by Taddeo di Bartolo signed and dated 1393 (or 1403?) This Sienese Gothic artist has depicted *Christ the Judge surrounded by Angels, Prophets, the Mother and St. John*. Lower down is the series of the *twelve Apostles*. The scene is linked to the two others painted on the façade end of the upper side-walls of the central nave which depict the *Blessed* and the *Damned*. Taddeo must have been helped by an assistant, whose crudely realistic, somewhat rustic style is specially discernible in the fantastic figures of the Damned and in the horrifying one of Satan, obviously intended to serve didactic ends, specially in the scene of the monstruous Demons tormenting the poor Sinners. Lower down, to the sides, further frescoed scenes of the *Assumption of the Virgin in Glory* (to the onlooker's left) and *St. Anthony Abbot* (right), all attributable to Benozzo Gozzoli.

The wall of the central nave facing onto the right aisle is frescoed with a lovely *St. Fina*, while the wall of the central nave facing onto the left aisle is depicted with a *St. Catherine of Alexandria*, both of which are considered the delicately sensitive handiwork of Lippo Memmi, painted some time after

RIGHT AISLE WALL

Scenes from the New Testament, by Barna da Siena.

1 – Annunciation
2 – Jesus enters Jerusalem
3 – The Last Supper
4 – Jesus on his way to Calvary
5 – Judas receives the thirty pieces of silver
6 – Nativity of Jesus
7 – Resurrection of Lazarus
8 – Jesus in the Garden of Gethsemane
9 – The Transfiguration
10 – The kiss of Judas
11 – Adoration of the Magi
12 – The wedding at Cana
13 – Jesus before Caiaphas
14 – Jesus receives St. Peter the Apostle
15 – The Flagellation of Jesus
16 – The Circumcision
17 – Jesus is christened
18 – Jesus crowned with the crown of thorns
19 – Jesus among the Doctors
20 – Jesus and the Women who loved Him
21 – The massacre of the Holy Innocents
22 – The Crucifixion
23 – The Flight into Egypt
24 – Frescoes damaged by the installation
     of a 16th century choir-loft

Annunciation, by Barna da Siena.

1320. Lippo, son of Memmo di Filippuccio, as we will mention further on, was brother-in-law to the great Simone Martini as well as being his closest and best assistant.

RIGHT AISLE. — The whole of the right wall of this aisle is covered with a magnificent cycle of frescoes that depict the *Stories from the New Testament*, arranged along several registers, centering around the *Crucifixion of Jesus*, that takes up two orders. The cycle is one of the most important examples of Italian Gothic art. Vasari, in his famous "Lives", mentions one master Barna (or Berna) da Siena, who, while painting these frescoes, says Vasari, fell from the scaffolding in 1381 and "in the space of two days departed this life". The cycle was therefore completed by Barna's follower, Giovanni d'Asciano. Recent studies have convinced researchers, however, that these frecoes were completed before the middle of the 14th century. Whether the painter Barna existed or not, the frescoes were certainly painted by a master of Simone Martini's circle, between 1333 and 1341 (a companion or "Chompagno", as the documents of the time reveal) whose stature must have become preeminent after Simone's departure for Avignon (1334) where he was to work at the papal court. The debate regarding the cycle of New Testament stories in San Gimignano and the works stylistically related to it is still open. On one hand, attempts have been made to attribute them to Lippo Memmi, who probably inherited his father Memmo di Filippuccio's position as "Pictor civicus" (Town painter) of San

Judas receiving the thirty pieces of silver, by Barna da Siena.

Gimignano. Another line of thought does not in any way disregard the evident points of contact with Lippo's work, but tends to consider the frescoes the handiwork of another artist, who might well have been the brother of Lippo, Federico (or Tederico) Memmi or even Donato Martini, Simone's brother. At any rate, the New Testament stories constitute the most exalted instance of the Memmi family's activity in San Gimignano and, as we have already stated, one of the noblest examples of Gothic art in Europe. If the great Simone Martini was the most refined and courtly interpreter of Gothic ideas, with his fluid lines and elegant forms, his "Chompagno" in San Gimignano used a massive, some what earthier and highly dramatic language, employing a profoundly moving tech-

Resurrection of Lazarus, by Barna da Siena.

nique, specially as regards the expressive qualities of his figures' faces. See for instance the piercing gaze of Judas in the episode of the *Kiss of Judas*, the dour, predatory expressions of the onlookers in the spectacular *Crucifixion* or the muttered comments on the lips of the priests in the *Pact of Judas*, the nobility of the Christ's head in the *Transfiguration* scene. Also, in the *Kiss of Judas* or in the scene of *Jesus on his way to Calvary*, we not only breathe a Giottoesque atmosphere, but also notice a striving after spatial depth, sometimes achieved thanks to the diagonals of the spears, torches or swaying ladders, or even more admirably by the continuous succession of the arched iron helms of the soldiers: it is a timelessly efficacious scene, that could have been

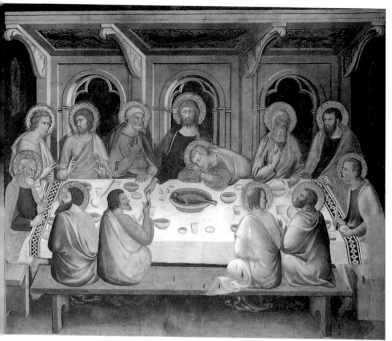

The Last Supper, by Barna da Siena.

painted today, thanks to a pictorial technique that reveals an awareness of detail that is akin to the ability of a "still-life" artist. As well as these hotly anxious sequences, this dramatically tense pathos, there is an almost musically fluid line which endows each scene with a simple, rustic elegance that cannot be said to achieve the refined sophistication of Simone Martini, but is certainly reminiscent of it.

The admirable tranquillity, the thoughtful serenity expressed in Jesus's face in the scene of *Jesus on his way to Calvary* or in the *Last Supper* are certainly Simonesque, as Simonesque as the *Annunciation*, which distinctly recalls the world-famous *Annunciation* painted by Simone for the Cathedral of Siena in 1333, which is now in the Uffizi Gallery in Florence. The San Gimignano *Annunciation* has an earthier feeling and the artist has included somewhat more naturalistic details, like the delightful figure of the little servant-girl, who has suddenly stopped spinning so that she can lay her ear to the wall and find out what the Virgin Mary is up to. We could go on thus ad infinitum, drawing attention to a thousand details that not only recall or differ from Simone's style, but reveal the San

Jesus on his way to Jerusalem, by Barna da Siena.

Gimignano master's familiarity with Giotto's monumental plasticity and Duccio di Buoninsegna's solemn, composed decorative refinement. This blending of influences is not fortuitous, inasmuch as San Gimignano is half way between Siena and Florence, which has, per force, led its artists to be influenced by the artistic trends of both of these famous Tuscan towns. The sequence of the scenes is described in the graph on page 13, which lists all the subjects depicted. Simone's "Chompagno" was also the author of the six great figures of *Prophets* above the six arches of the right aisle, opposite the New Testament stories we have just described. Above the last arch, opposite the Chapel of St. Fina, which we

St. Gregory announcing her imminent death to St. Fina, by a master of the Duccio circle.

are about to observe, is an early 14th century fresco by a master of the Duccio circle, which recalls the style of Niccolò di Segna, depicting *St. Gregorius telling St. Fina of her imminent death*. A beautiful carved and inlaid *bench* by master Antonio da Colle (c. 1470) runs the length of the wall beneath the New Testament scenes.

CHAPEL OF ST. FINA. — At the end of the aisle, fenced in by a 19th century *grille* and a marble *balustrade* made in 1661, is the Chapel of St. Fina, where the bones of the patron saint of San Gimignano, who died on the 12 March 1253, lie beneath the altar. This exquisite Florentine Renaissance architectural jewel was designed by Giuliano da Maiano, who was charged with the task by the authorities of the Cathedral in 1488. The chapel was consecrated in 1488 as proved by the inscription on the right pilaster. Even the materials used in the chapel reflect the early Renaissance tenets of the Florentine architectural tradition and remind one of the old Sacristy in San Lorenzo or the Pazzi Chapel by Filippo Brunelleschi or the other delicately perfect creations by Rossellino, Michelozzo or Giuliano da Maiano himself. Geometrical perfection characterizes the pietra serena walls, highlighted by richly classical decoration

The altar of St. Fina, by Benedetto and Giuliano da Maiano (detail).

on the capitals, and on the semi-pillars and cherub heads in the friezes outlined in gold-leaf. The decoration, together with the altar (1472-1477) is by Giuliano da Maiano's brother, Benedetto, one of the most famous Florentine Renaissance sculptors. In order to enrich the decoration further, the master used marble instead of pietra serena and pushed back the altar, placing it below the great arch at the end of the chapel; moreover in order to achieve more of a scenographic effect, he sculpted two looped-back hangings in the marble overlaying the arch, highlighting them with gold-leaf. The complex was unfortunately restructured in 1738 and somewhat arbitrarily re-arranged in 1881. The marble altarpiece above the altar surrounds a golden grille that shelters the reliquary containing St. Fina's head. Benedetto da Maiano carved three little scenes in low relief into the architrave, describing: *St. Gregory announcing St. Fina's imminent death to her*; the *burial of the saint*, and the *miracle of the dead man brought back to life*. A charming *Madonna and Child* flanked by *two angels* in an almond-shaped frame of cherub-heads crowns the whole. The perfection of these decorative elements would in

Chapel of St. Fina, by Benedetto and Giuliano da Maiano.

effect have been sufficient on their own, but it was decided to cover the walls, pendentives and the vault with frescoed illustrations of the life of the saint.

Domenico Bigordi, better known as Ghirlandaio, together with his brother David and his brother-in-law, Sebastiano Mainar-

St. Gregory announces her imminent death to St. Fina, by Domenico Ghirlandaio.

di, a citizen of San Gimignano, frescoed the two side-walls with the great scenes showing *St. Gregory, Pope, appearing to Fina as she lay sick and telling her of her imminent death; the burial of St. Fina*. The former is less spectacular, more intimate and peaceful, with the girl lying on her wooden pallet, attended by her nurse Beldia and Donna Bonaventura. The perfect perspective of the bare little chamber enhances each separate item and transforms it into something infinitely precious, as if the whole composition were a kind of "still-life": from the great platter to the wine-flask and glass, to the fruit on its dish, to the inscription on the end-wall next to the window, that frames a landscape brimming with light. The Burial Scene is more pompous: prelates, populace and nobles surround the body of the young girl lying on her bier. The semi-circle formed by the figures is echoed by the niche of the apse extending back

The Burial of St. Fina, by Domenico Ghirlandaio.

behind them, transforming the scene into an open, airy composition set-off by the enchanting views of San Gimignano each side of the apse, that Ghirlandaio uses as a backdrop for the whole. The three portraits placed beneath the towers on the left are almost certainly to be identified as Ghirlandaio himself with his two assistants, mentioned above. Ghirlandaio has also managed to include a number of episodes that popular legend connects with St. Fina's death: the little blind altar boy who regains his sight upon touching the body of the saint, her nurse, Beldia whose wasted, useless hand is miraculously healed, while the bells are set ringing by angelic hands. The frescoes on the vault, much damaged, still reveal the figures of *evangelists, holy bishops* and *prophets*. Beneath the two side-wall frescoes a pair of lovely *inlaid benches* by Antonio da Colle (15th century). The *reliquary of St. Fina*, that

The Burial of St. Fina, by Domenico Ghirlandaio (detail of the left side of the scene).

is, as we have already said, situated in the centre of the altar, is considered a masterpiece of Sienese early 14th century craftsmanship, being a blend of sculpture, painting and goldsmithery. The head of the girl is painted, while her robe, richly

The Burial of St. Fina, by Domenico Ghirlandaio (detail of the right side of the scene).

encrusted with ancient multicoloured glass, together with her lovely cascade of hair is covered in gleaming gold-leaf.

At the centre of the transept, the *high altar* restored more than once, was totally re-made in 1937 in a badly imitated Romanes-

Above: **two prophets, attributed to Mainardi** (Chapel of St. Fina), *below*: **reliquary bust of St. Fina;** *right*: **detail of St. Gregory announcing her imminent death to St. Fina, by Ghirlandaio.**

que style. At the same time, the lovely marble *Ciborium* flanked by two angels, carved by Benedetto da Maiano in 1475, was replaced on top of the renovated altar. The wooden *Crucifix* above the altar was sculpted by G. Antonio Noferi of Florence, in 1754.

Immaculate Conception, by Ludovico Cardi, known as Cigoli.

The Birth of the Virgin, by Pier Dandini.

LEFT AISLE. — The *Chapel of the Immaculate Conception*, frescoed by Pier Dandini (18th cent.) with scenes depicting the *Coronation of the Virgin* (on the ceiling vault), the *Birth of the Virgin* and the *Adoration of the Annunciate Madonna* (side-walls), is an imitation of the Chapel of St. Fina. Above the altar, a fine canvas depicting the *Immaculate Virgin*, painted by the Florentine, Ludovico Cardi, known as Cigoli, from the name of his birthplace.

The ancient *baptismal font*, carved by Giovanni di Cecco (Cecchino della Pietra), at present in the loggia of the Baptistery (see page. 36), will be placed beside the Chapel of the Immaculate Conception. The wall of the left aisle is completely covered with frescoed *Scenes from the Old Testament*, painted in 1367 by the Sienese, Bartolo di Fredi, as indicated by the signature and date on the lower frieze left of the central scene.

LEFT AISLE WALL

Scenes from the Old Testament, by Bartolo di Fredi

1 – Creation of the World
2 – Adam and Eve being driven out of the Garden of Eden
3 – Joseph has his brethren put in prison
4 – Cain slays Abel
5 – Joseph is recognized by his brethren
6 – The Creation of Man
7 – Noah builds the Ark
8 – Moses transforms the staff into a serpent.
9 – The animals enter the Ark
10 – The crossing of the Red Sea
11 – Adam in the Garden of Eden
12 – Noah thanks the Lord upon emerging from the Ark
13 – The drunkenness of Noah
14 – Moses on Mount Sinai
15 – Creation of Eve
16 – Abraham and Lot on their way to the land of Canaan
17 – The Lord allows Satan to tempt Job
18 – Abraham parts from Lot
19 – Job's servants and flocks destroyed by Satan
20 – The forbidden fruit
21 – Joseph's dream
22 – Satan causes Job's house to collapse, burying his children
23 – Joseph is lowered into the well by his brethren
24 – Job thanks the Lord
25 – Frescoes damaged by the installation of the organ in 1501
26 – Job is struck by sickness

Abraham parts from Lot, by Bartolo di Fredi.

Bartolo di Fredi imbued these imaginatively depicted scenes with his own particular brand of blythe freshness, providing a very personal view of the biblical stories and enriching the scenes with lively, unexpected detail. See, for instance, the bloody massacre of Pharoah's army in the *Crossing of the Red Sea* or the *Cortège of the Jewish people who escaped slavery*, which is a veritable itemized dictionary of the costumes of the period. The *Creation of the World* offers a fascinating insight into the astronomical tenets of the 14th century, with the terrestrial sphere placed in the centre of the great blue celestial circle, divided into its twelve Zodiac sections. The animals with *Adam in the Garden of Eden* and in the scene of

The Lord allows Satan to tempt Job, by Bartolo di Fredi.

Noah's burnt offering are of extremely high quality, whilst the episode of *Joseph and his brethren* is more intimate. One of the most fascinating scenes is the one showing *Job in his prosperity about to be tempted by Satan*, where the exquisitely drafted lines and the precisely described figures around Job's banqueting table reveal the skill of an illuminator (the musical instruments are of extraordinary interest) and recall the Sienese painting tradition of Bartolo's time which led up to the frescoes of the *Effects of Good Government* by Ambrogio Lorenzetti in the Hall of Peace in the Palazzo Pubblico in Siena. Lastly, the scene of the *Earthquake destroying Job's Children's House* is the vivid, simple description of a building suddenly collapsing over the heads of its inmates who appear

The servants of Job are slaughtered, by Bartolo di Fredi.

to be trapped by pieces of stone and rafters of such delicate consistency that even a fly would surely escape unscathed from their falling on top of it. An unsophisticated candour, perhaps a little too narrative in style, however gives life and credibility to the stories that succeed each other in their sections and order, according to the scheme we include a graph of on page 30. The last scenes of the cycle were lost, in the 15th century, when the *choir-loft* was walled into the left wall. Against the wall, two magnificent inlaid *benches*, which could be attributed to Antonio da Colle or perhaps to his son Bartolomeo. Opposite Bartolo di Fredi's frescoes, above the arches dividing the left aisle from the nave, runs a frieze of *Prophets*, by Pier Francesco Fiorentino (c. 1474).

Satan causes the house of Job's children to collapse upon them, by Bartolo di Fredi.

THE SACRISTIES. — There are some exceptionally fine paintings in the *Sacristies*, all by Florentine masters of the 17th and 18th centuries. See for instance *Christ descending into Limbo*, by Matteo Rosselli (1578-1650); *Coronation of the Virgin*, by Domenico Cresti, called Passignano (1560-1636); a *Nativity* and an *Adoration of the Trinity*, by another Florentine, whose name was probably Camillo Sacrestani; a *Deposition from the Cross*, by the already mentioned Domenico Passignano and another *Coronation of the Virgin*, by Matteo Rosselli. Outside the Cathedral of the Collegiata, one walks immediately right, through an archway surmounted by a 14th century statue of *St. Gimignano* (of a somewhat rustic flavour), into Piazza Pecori.

Deposition from the Cross, by Domenico Cresti, known as Passignano.

The little cloister of the Collegiata, seen from piazza Pecori.

PIAZZA PECORI

To ones right is an ex-cloister, transformed into an oratory in 1632 and subsquently used as a baptistery. Since the recent re-opening of the arches, the oratory has resumed its loggia-like character and can also be entered via the door that leads out of the church's left aisle, beneath the choir-loft, next to the Chapel of the Immaculate Conception. At the end of the loggia, one can admire a frescoed *Annunciation*, which can better be attributed to Sebastiano Mainardi, than to his brother-in-law Ghirlandaio (1482). The *baptismal font*, sculpted by Giovanni di Cecco (Cecchino della Pietra), is still standing beneath the fresco as we go into print, but will be transferred into the Collegiata Cathedral (see page 29). There is a *Baptism of the Christ* on the central panel of the font and two *Agnus Dei* on the others. The font is signed by the Sienese artist and dated 1379. The older ceiling vault of the loggia reveals traces of a frescoed figure of a *prophet* that can be attributed to the "Chompagno" of Simone, who painted the New Testament

Above: **the baptismal font of the Collegiata;** *below:* **Annunciation, attributed to Sebastiano Mainardi.**

Stories inside the Cathedral. The great Renaissance *niche* in grey "pietra serena" was carved by Girolamo di Cecchino in 1472. The old buildings on the other side of the little square, once used as the "Chaplains' Dormitory" now house the *Museum of Religious Art* and the *Archaeological Museum*.

Piazza Pecori (the Museum of Religious Art is on the right, not in view).

MUSEUM OF RELIGIOUS ART

Ground Floor. VESTIBULE and CHAPEL. — This is where a large number of stone or marble items are displayed, which used either to be in the Collegiata or in other religious buildings in the San Gimignano area. See for instance: the *badges*, *tomb-stones*, *column-bearing lions*, *water-stoups*, *reliefs* and even a (15th century?) *chair* used by the wet-nurses during the baptisms. A number of 14th and 15th century objects

Left: **St. Anthony Abbot, attributed to Francesco di Valdambrino**; *right*: **Madonna of the Rose, by Bartolo di Fredi** (Museum of Religious Art).

complete the collection. There is also a fine painted wooden *Crucifix* above the chapel altar, which is either late 14th or early 15th century.

Upstairs. 1st ROOM TO THE RIGHT. — A very rare *carpet*, most likely not of Persian, but of Egyptian provenance from the Mameluke epoch (16th or early 17th century); a *Holy Family*: a late 16th century copy of the original by Andrea del Sarto; a wooden *pulpit* with little figures cut into the panels (15th or 16th century); a *Christ at the Column* (small 17th century

Detail of the altar-front of the Golden Doves, (Museum of Religious Art).

copy in painted wood of Michelangelo's Christ in Santa Maria sopra Minerva in Rome); a *Decollation of St. John*, a canvas signed and dated by "I Bonelli" 1624; wooden *bench* attributed to Bartolommeo da Colle (15th century).

1st ROOM TO THE LEFT. — Great, important painted wooden *Crucifix* by 13th century Sienese master, reminiscent of others, all Romanesque in style, which can be compared to the famous "Volto Santo" in the Lucca Cathedral (end of 12th, beginning of 13th century), all probably derived from some c. 8th century Syrian prototype; two painted wooden statues of an *Announcing Angel* and the upper portion of a *Virgin Annunciate* (14th century) by a master of the Sienese-Pisan school, once in the Collegiata and replaced by the two statues of the Angel and the Virgin by Jacopo della Quercia now in front of the Benozzo Gozzoli fresco of St. Sebastian; a marble *bust of Onofrio di Pietro*, rector of the Cathedral works, sculpted in 1493 by

St. Gimignano enthroned, from an illuminated codex, by Niccolò di Ser Sozzo (Museum of Religious Art).

Benedetto da Maiano; *Madonna and Child with Saints*, attributed to Vincenzo Tamagni (16th century); marble *head* of a *Christ*, attributed to Pietro Torrigiani, Michelangelo's rival (c. 1498-1500); bust of the *Redeemer*, in terracotta, also by Torrigiani; painted wooden statue of *St. Anthony Abbot*, attributed to Francesco di Valdambrino, one of Jacopo della Quercia's assistants; marble *Shroud-bearing Angel*, attributed to the great Sienese sculptor Goro di Gregorio, c. 1330; another sculpted (headless) *angel*, also attributed to Goro di Gregorio.

The long room of the Archaeological Museum.

IInd ROOM. — The *Madonna of the Rose* (Madonna and Child, holding a rose in his hand), an exquisite, late 14th century painting by Bartolo di Fredi who seems to evoke the chromatic splendour of the great Sienese masters of the early 14th century in this last, superbly delicate reminiscence of Simone Martini, Pietro or Ambrogio Lorenzetti; the *Golden Doves' Altarfront*, a vermilion velvet altarfront embroidered in gold thread, a rare and distinguished 15th century masterpiece (it was first made in 1449, but was later enlarged in 1466); a

Two views of the Archaeological Museum.

terracotta relief of a *Madonna and Child*, a replica among a considerable number of others, all of which probably came from Lorenzo Ghiberti's workshop (15th century); a detached frescoed *St. Lucy*, attributed to Lippo Memmi and much akin to the two frescoes attributed to this master on the counter-façade of the Cathedral; *St. Gregory* (sinopia of a fresco) from the Chapel of St. Fina and attributed to Sebastiano Mainardi.

IIIrd or TREASURE ROOM. — A large number of *silver objects* (14th-18th centuries), that used to be part of the liturgical paraphernalia of the Cathedral or of the other churches of the district, are displayed in a series of show-cases. Admirable *liturgical garments* (15th-18th centuries) in other show-cases. The *illuminated manuscripts* and *codexes* that have been recovered after a recent theft will also be displayed in this room. Among the admirable illuminated miniatures let us mention those painted by the Sienese masters Lippo Vanni and Niccolò di Ser Sozzo (14th century).

ARCHAEOLOGICAL MUSEUM. — A large number of archaeological finds from the area around San Gimignano have been placed in a large chamber and are to be better displayed in future. Most of the objects come from the Etruscan tombs of the district (*plates, bowls, vases, lamps, axes, spears, mirrors, golden rings, stone sarcophagi*, etc.).

The Palace of the Commune and the Loggia to its left.

PALACE OF THE COMMUNE

Back in the Cathedral square, let us now cast a more attentive glance on the Palace of the Commune, to our right. It was started towards the end of the 13th century and enlarged around the middle of the following century. According to a

The courtyard of the Palace of the Commune.

fairly ill-founded tradition, the architect responsible for its design is supposed to have been Arnolfo di Cambio, the great Florentine master (born in nearby Colle Val d'Elsa).

The so-called Haranguing Podium (*Arringo*) sticks out from the façade on the right beneath the great tower and is led up to by two flights of steps from the sides; it was from this podium that the Podestà (governor) swore fealty to the statutes. To the right of the palace is the so-called Great Tower (*Torre Grossa*), entirely built in travertine and, as we have already said, 54 metres high; it was completed in 1311. Left of the building, is the great double-arched *loggia* that was completed in 1347 and restored to its original appearance in 1934 (after it had been walled-up in the 16th century). This is where a 14th century Sienese School fresco, detached from a dismantled chapel and depicting a *Madonna and Child between Saints Michael Archangel and John the Baptist*, was placed.

One enters the palace through a narrow passage, which leads into a *courtyard* that was part of the 14th century additions. It was chiefly built in brick and decorated with a number of frescoed Podestà badges and crests belonging to the governors who resided in the palace. At the end of the courtyard is a *Cistern* bearing the arms of Podestà Alberti (1361) which ensured the water supply of the palace. It is made of travertine and is reminiscent of the better known one in the middle of the appropriately named Piazza della Cisterna (square of the cistern). A great portico or "Loggia of the Judge" (Giudice) opens off the right side of the courtyard from which the judge dispensed justice. The loggia is decorated with fine frescoes, such as the one depicting *St. Ive*, patron saint of lawyers, *dispensing Justice* to the humble folk, whilst a number of rich people outside the chamber are endeavouring to enter, bearing rich gifts. The monochrome fresco is justly attributed to Antonio Bazzi, known as Sodoma, the famous Sienese master (albeit born in Vercelli), who followed in the footsteps of his master Leonardo da Vinci. This fresco, which was partly painted together with Vincenzo Tamagni (a San Gimignano painter and helper of Sodoma), must have been painted around 1507, which was when Nicolò Machiavelli was Florentine ambassador in San Gimignano: which explains the crest of the Machiavelli family supported by two cherubs in front of

Left: **the cistern of the courtyard;** *right*: **the little loggia leading to the entrance of the Civic Museum.**

46

Above: **St. Ive dispensing justice;** *below*: **the Judge dismissing Falsehood, both attributed to Sodoma.**

47

Dante's Hall (Palace of the Commune).

the dais St. Ive is seated upon. The second fresco in the loggia shows a *Madonna and Child between Saints Gregory and Gimignano* — a late 14th century work, which reminds one of Lippo Vanni's style. The third fresco is a kind of allegory of *Justice* showing a *Judge dismissing Falsehood, flanked by Prudence* (with a serpent) *and Truth* (the naked girl). The style of this fresco is reminiscent of Sodoma's St. Ive. The second bay contains another fresco depicting *St. Catherine and a Holy Bishop* (14th century). Above the archway leading into the courtyard there is a mediocre modern fresco, in definite contrast with the other fine works, depicting the *Virtues of Prudence, Justice and Fortitude*. A steep flight of steps and an elegant little loggia lead up to the reception rooms of the Palace of the Commune, which are now occupied by the *Civic Museum* (Museo Civico). Here we find a considerable number of old Sienese and Florentine paintings (from the 12th to the 15th centuries). In the corridor, there is a "sinopia" (the sketch underlying a fresco) of a *Madonna and Child with a lion* (early 14th century).

DANTE'S HALL. — This is the great General Council Hall, where on the 8th May 1300, Dante Alighieri, as Florentine ambassador, urged the citizens of San Gimignano to join the

**The great Enthroned Madonna and Child with saints (Maestà),
by Lippo Lemmi** (Dante's Hall).

Guelph league. The hall is dominated by a great *Madonna and
Child enthroned* (Maestà), surrounded by a crowd of angels
and saints and venerated by the kneeling Podestà Nello di
Mino dei Tolomei, who commissioned the work, as demon-
strated by the inscription: "AT THE TIME OF MASTER
NELLO OF MASTER MINO DE' TOLOMEI OF SIENA, HO-
NOURABLE PODESTÀ AND CAPTAIN OF THE COMMUNE
AND OF THE PEOPLE OF THE LANDS OF SAN GIMIG-
NANO MCCCXVII". The great fresco is thus dated 1317 and
signed by Lippo Memmi, close helper and brother-in-law to
Simone Martini: "LIPPUS MEMI DE SENIS ME PINXIT". The
nobility of the style, adorned with gleaming leaf-gold and the
richly decorated garments of the holy personages in the scene,
is distinctly reminiscent of the world-famous *Enthroned
Madonna and Child*, that Simone Martini painted in 1315 for
the great Map Room in Siena's Palazzo Pubblico. Lippo
Memmi's Maestà was also enlarged in the second half of the
14th century, when the two paired figures of *Saints Anthony
Abbot* and *Fina* (left) and *Bartolo* and *Louis IX* (right) joined the
reverent throng. They were almost certainly painted by Bartolo di Fredi. An inscription on the right step, however, bears
the name of the 15th century Florentine painter, Benozzo
Gozzoli: "BENOZIOUS FLORENTINUS PICTOR RESTAU-

49

Detail of Lippo Memmi's Maestà (Dante's Hall).

RAVIT ANNO DOMINI MCCCCLXVII" and as the faces of St. Bartolo and St. Louis closely remind one of Benozzo's style, one is led to conclude that he was almost certainly responsible for the restoration of this part of the fresco as well as for the blue of the sky in the background and for the gold on the throne of the Madonna. Dante's hall also contains other frescoes with *hunting scenes, tourneys, allegorical figures* and, at the end, a fine scene, probably to be identified as a *Homage payed to King Charles of Anjou*. It was certainly painted before 1292, because in that year an inscription was placed over a section of the fresco, recalling a judgement issued by Scolaio Ardinghelli, Bishop of Tyre and Arborea, regarding a controversy between the lay and religious spheres of power.

A jousting knight (Dante's Hall).

Next to Dante's Hall, is the *Secret Assembly Hall*; here we find a bust of *St. Bartholomew*, in a niche, attributed, without any particular supportive evidence, to an almost unknown Giovanni Gonnelli, known as the "Blind man of Gambassi"; it is at any rate a 15th century, probably Sienese, work. In the room next-door, there is another painted terracotta bust of an old man (perhaps the *Blessed Bartolo*) of impressive realism, attributed to a late 15th century Florentine master of the circle of Pietro Torrigiani. Another niche contains a stone statue of *St. James the Apostle* (17th century). Beyond the landing, a little room in the tower, on the other side of Dante's hall, contains a 16th century *mortar*, as well as a magnificent and very rare 14th century *war-helm*.

After the first flight of steps, one comes (on the left) to the ex-*Chapel of the Podestà*, containing a great fresco of the *Trinity* (Crucifix, Dove and the Father) framed by six smaller scenes, dated 1497 and attributed to Pier Francesco Fiorentino, in the last, rather weary style of his old age.

51

The first room of the Civic Museum.

CIVIC MUSEUM

1st ROOM. — Here we find a number of important works from public and religious buildings in the town. Starting from the right: great *Crucifix*, on the sides of which are painted *Scenes from the Passion*, by the Florentine Coppo di Marcovaldo (c. 1260), one of the most important 13th century Tuscan works. Above it a small frescoed *Madonna and Child*, by the Florentine Cenno di Francesco di Ser Cenni (c. 1413). *Enthroned Madonna and Child* with the small figures of *St. Augustine* and *St. Juliana*: an important piece, unfortunately mostly indescipherable, by a 13th century Sienese master, probably Guido da Siena (1270); *Madonna and Child between Saints Bartholomew and Anthony Abbot*, with the donor *Tommaso Cortesi*, painted on panel, with predella, dated 1490, by Pier Francesco Fiorentino; *Madonna and Child in glory, with Saints Augustine, Gimignano, Mary Magdalen, Fina, John the Baptist and Jerome*, by Sebastiano Mainardi, Ghirlandaio's follower; *Madonna of Humility with Saints Andrew and Prosperus*, dated 1466 and signed Benozzo Gozzoli. On the end wall: two round panels showing the *Angel* and the *Virgin Annunciate*, delicate masterpieces by Filippino Lippi (1482); *Madonna in glory with Saints Gregory and Benedict in adoration*, painted in 1512, by Bernardino di Betto, better known as Pinturicchio, for Fra

Great Crucifix, by Coppo di Marcovaldo (Civic Museum).

Giovanni da Verona. One of the most luminous paintings ever produced by the Umbrian master, who is renowned for having worked both in Siena and Rome. Continuing along the left wall: *Madonna and Child enthroned flanked by Saints Gregory, John the Baptist, Francis and Fina*, attributed to Domenico di Michelino, a follower of Fra Angelico; *Madonna and Child with Saints John the Baptist, Mary Magdalen, Augustine and Martha*, dated 1466 and signed by Benozzo Gozzoli; *Madonna and Child*, by unknown Sienese master (c. 1270); painted, late 13th century Sienese *Crucifix*, attributed to the so-called

Madonna and Child with saints, by Benozzo Gozzoli (Civic Museum).

"Master of the Clarissan Order", because of a painted panel by him in the Clarissan convent in Siena.

IInd ROOM. — Wooden *shrine* with doors, which used to house the reliquary of St. Fina. It is painted on both sides. The front shows *St. Gregory* and *St. Fina* holding the town of San Gimignano with all its towers and surrounded by its walls. On the inner side of the doors, the first four stories from the life of St. Fina, from the top right: *The saint in her sickness assisted by*

Madonna in glory with Saints Gregory and Benedict, by Pinturicchio (Civic Museum).

her mother, while a man endeavors to chase away the mice from her chamber; the Devil causes St. Fina's mother to fall downstairs; the citizens of San Gimignano pay homage to the body of

Left: **St. Gimignano** (detail), **by Taddeo di Bartolo;** *right*: **Madonna and Child with saints, by Sebastiano Mainardi;** *below*: **Angel and Virgin Annunciate, by Filippino Lippi** (Civic Museum).

Fina, while the mice are transformed into violets; Beldia, Fina's nurse, has her wasted hand healed by touching Fina's body, which is being taken to be buried. The rear doors show two angels flanked by the following scenes: the *healing of a possessed man; a mason who has fallen from a roof is saved; a*

Above: **a room in the Civic Museum;** *below:* **Tabernacle of St. Fina, by Lorenzo di Nicolò di Martino** (Civic Museum).

ship is rescued; St. Fina's shirt extinguishes a fire that had broken out in San Gimignano. This entrancing creation, with its sparkling gold leaf and jewel-like colours, is unanimously attributed to Lorenzo di Niccolò di Martino, a Florentine helper of Niccolò di Pietro Gerini and can be dated around the end of the 14th, beginning of the 15th centuries; painted *Cross* by Sienese master (with Florentine reminiscences) of the end of the 13th century; *Madonna and Child enthroned with Saints*

Peter, John the Evangelist, Catherine, Agnes, John the Baptist, Michael, Francis and Clare; an important piece as regards the development of Sienese art in San Gimignano: attributable to Memmo di Filippuccio, c. 1310; fragment of fresco by Bartolo di Fredi (end of 14th century) showing a number of *female heads*; *Madonna and Child*, by Lorenzo di Niccolò di Martino; *Madonna of Humility*, attributed to the Master of San Jacopo a Mucciano (late 14th/early 15th century); *bell* dated 1487.

IIIrd ROOM. — *Madonna and Child with angels*, attributed to Sebastiano Mainardi — a great polyptych, showing the *Madonna and Child with Saints Nicholas of Bari, Christopher, John the Evangelist, and Gimignano* in the central panel — in the pendentives: *Annunciation, Christ blessing*, and the *Saints Peter and Paul* — a work signed by the late 14th century Sienese master Taddeo di Bartolo; *Madonna and Child between Saints Justus and Thomas* and the donor, *friar Tommaso Cortesi*, by Pier Francesco Fiorentino; *Madonna and Child*, fresco, dated 1528, from the workshop of Sebastiano Mainardi; *Madonna and Child*, by the 15th century Florentine master, Neri di Bicci (c. 1460-70); *Madonna and Child with angels and Saints Catherine of Alexandria, Nicholas of Bari, Ludovic and Peter the Martyr*, a small altar-piece, attributed to Jacopo da Firenze, active between the end of the 14th century and the beginning of the 15th; the *Altarpiece of St. Gimignano*, showing the enthroned saint blessing the town on his knees — on the central panel, flanked on either side by eight episodes from the life of the saint: *Vision of St. Severus during the burial of St. Gimignano*; the *saint prevents a storm from breaking over the church where a service is being said over his grave*; *St. Gimignano orders Attila to lift his siege on the mythical town of Silvia* (the name of San Gimignano in Roman times); *the saint causes the outlaws who were besieging Silvia to leave*; *the saint dismisses the Devil, who was awaiting his return to the church after his temporary absence from it*; *Gratian finds out from the Devil that only St. Gimignano can exorcise his possessed daughter*; *on his way to Constantinople, he calms a sea-storm*; *the saint exorcises a possessed woman*: the great panel, once in the Collegiata, should be attributed to the late 14th century Sienese, Taddeo di Bartolo. *Madonna and Child with Sts. Catherina of Alexandria, Nicholas of Bari, Fina and Anthony Abbot*, attributed to Jacopo da Firenze (late 14th century); a dismembered polyptych with the *Assumption of the Virgin, venerated by Sts. Catherine of Alexandria, Bartholomew, Benedict and Thomas the Apostle*: a very fine work by the Sienese, Niccolò di Ser Sozzo (c. 1345), a painter noted for his remarkably fine illumination work, which includes the marvellous

Madonna and Child, by Sebastiano Mainardi (Civic Museum).

Assumption of the Virgin in Glory on the cover page of the Caleffo book at the State Archives of Siena, which is in fact known as the "Caleffo of the Assumption" (Caleffo dell'Assunta); *polyptych of St. Julian*; the *enthroned saint between St. Anthony Abbot and St. Martin*, an elegant piece by the unknown "Master of 1419", thus named after another panel by him, today in London, dated that year; *St. Bartholomew the Apostle enthroned*, flanked by four episodes from his life: *he is stolen away by the Devil as soon as he is born*; he *refuses to adore idols; he is flayed alive; he is beheaded* — the triptych is attributed to Lorenzo di Niccolò di Martino and is dated 1401; *Madonna and Child with St. John the Baptist as a child*, on a round panel, once attributed to Mainardi, but now thought to be by his follower, Bartolommeo di Giovanni (15th century).

Scenes of sexual initiation, attributed to Memmo di Filippuccio
(Civic Museum).

THE CHAMBER OF THE PODESTÀ. — One of the tower rooms, fascinatingly decorated with frescoes which are unique because of the theme they develop: probably the sexual initiation of a young man: *the young man whose mother* (?) *is trying to hold him back is led into a tent* (or whorehouse?), *from which he is chased out by persons brandishing sticks* (or spindles) (didn't he have enough money to pay?); *the youth with a friend courts a damsel while walking the streets of the town; the damsel and the young man bathe naked in a big wooden bath-tub; the youth is shown by a woman* (procuress?) *into a girl's bed-chamber and gets into bed with her*; other scene difficult to interpret. On the lower register, other scenes of a moralistic, anti-sexual-love tone: *Campaste riding the philosopher Aristotle and whipping him; two young lovers reading a book*, (could they be Paolo and Francesca, who were killed by the latter's husband?) — the frescoes are rightly attributed to Memmo di Filippuccio, who, as we have already stated, was father to Federico and Lippo Memmi, the brother-in-law and closest helper of Simone Martini — they were probably painted around the beginning of the 14th century; fine painted wooden *reliquary* of *St. Fina* showing the head and bust of the saint, lately attributed to the Sienese sculptor Mariano d'Angelo Romanelli, who was active at the end of the 14th century in Siena; altarpiece showing a *Madonna and Child with Sts.*

Above: **young lovers bathing together;** *below:* **the youth about to get into the young damsel's bed, frescoes attributed to Memmo di Filippuccio** (Civic Museum).

Gimignano, Augustine and the donor, by Pier Francesco Fiorentino; *Madonna and Child,* fresco by the same Pier Francesco, c. 1480-'90.

The famous Cistern in the square named after it (Piazza della Cisterna).

PIAZZA DELLA CISTERNA

Leading off the Cathedral square, is the so-called Piazza della Cisterna (erstwhile Piazza delle Taverne) which is the ancient commercial centre of the town. In the middle, an old well or *cistern*, an octagonal travertine structure, first built in 1237 and entirely re-built in 1346 during the governorship of Podestà Guccio Malavolti, whose crest (a ladder) is carved onto both sides of the well-ring. The whole square, which is certainly the most picturesque in the town, is surrounded by medieval buildings on which the whitish-grey travertine alternates with the russetty bricks. Starting from the left, upon leaving the Cathedral square: in the corner, we find the 15th century *Palazzo Cortesi-Lolli*, at present housing the Monte dei Paschi di Siena bank. The narrow *Vicolo dell'Oro* takes its name from the workshops of the goldsmiths, the craftsmen of

Piazza della Cisterna.

great repute, who used, among other things to beat out the impalpably thin sheets of pure gold employed by the painters for the gleaming backgrounds of the magnificent polyptychs which were placed on the altars of the churches. Next comes *Palazzo Lupi* with its robustly structured *Torre del Diavolo* (Devil's Tower), which owes its name to the fact that its owner, once returning from a long voyage, found it taller than he had left it and concluded that the Devil must have finished

Left: **the Devil's tower (Torre del Diavolo);** *right:* **the twin-mullioned Gothic windows of Palazzo Tortoli.**

building it. On the other side of the square, there is a succession of buildings, all differing from each other, some in travertine, some in brick, whose architectural variety is harmonised by the use of similar materials, producing an entrancing effect of strength and simplicity. They used to belong to the ancient families of the Cetti and the Braccieri, and are nowadays put to the most varied uses. *Palazzo Tortoli*, at the end (set against the squat *Torre dei Pucci*), is of great charm, with its narrow, mullioned, Gothic windows and its façade enlivened by its red and white materials. This side of the square is concluded by the so-called *Arch of the Becci and Cugnanesi*, beyond which, as we shall see, Via San Giovanni starts its descent. The *Becci Tower* is immediately in front of the arch, while the *Cugnanesi Tower* is immediately behind it. The arch itself is in effect the Southern Gate of the ancient walls of the town. A further succession of medieval buildings lead up to the Loggia of the Palace of the Commune. The twin *towers*, just before the said Loggia, used to belong to the *Ardinghelli* family.

From Piazza della Cisterna, one walks down *Via del Castello*, leaving the Devil's Tower to our left and Palazzo Tortoli to our right, and one reaches the *Castle* (Castello).

64

SECOND ITINERARY ·

From the Cathedral square to Piazza della Cisterna — Via di Castello — The Castle and the Fortress (Rocca) — San Lorenzo in Ponte — Porta alle Fonti (Springs) — St. Fina's house — Via San Giovanni

Bird's eye-view of the Castle, which is used at present as a prison.

THE CASTLE AND THE FORTRESS

The building used to be the powerful stronghold of the Bishop of Volterra, who, between the 10th and 11th centuries, ruled over the first core of San Gimignano; after the fall of the Bishop from power, the Castle became the Fortress that defended the youthful Commune from the beginning of the 13th century until 1353, when Florence, after having defeated the town, decided to build a second Fortress, on the hill of Montestaffoli, just above the Cathedral. Only a few shattered remains are left of this *Fortress* (Rocca) but its highest point offers one of the most beautiful views of the towers of San

Above: detail of the walls of the "Rocca" (Fortress); *below*: view of the garden of the Fortress.

Above: the Fortress seen from the tower of the Palace of the Commune; *below*: view of the towers, from the Fortress.

The eastern side of San Lorenzo in Ponte.

Gimignano. The much more ancient Castle was thus abandoned and was later taken over by the Dominican order who transformed it into a monastery, the Chapel of which is still in good condition, with its great carved and gilded wooden Baroque altar. Towards the end of the 18th century, the Dominicans moved out and in due course the Castle became a men's prison (1844). This great structure, however, will shortly be restored. One of the most recent discoveries in the centre of the courtyard is an Etruscan hypogeum (underground tomb). A new prison has just been built outside the town and one hopes that the ancient complex will be put to more culturally appropriate uses in the not too distant future.

Next to the Castle, at the end of Via San Giovanni, we find the much altered and restored *Church of San Lorenzo in Ponte* (at the Bridge), a Romanesque structure, built in 1240. It has no side-aisles and the raised choir has a vaulted roof. On the walls, a cycle of frescoed *Stories of St. Benedict* is still fairly legible, whilst a great scene of the *Damned* is unfortunately much damaged, the apse semicircle contains an equally extensive frescoed scene showing *Christ in Glory with the Madonna and the twelve Apostles*; the style which is still very Gothic, is that of the Florentine, Cenni di Francesco di Ser

Madonna and Child in glory with angels, attributed to Simone Martini and restored by Cenni di Francesco (two details); *below*: vases from the Hospital of St. Fina (San Lorenzo in Ponte).

The ancient Springs (Fonti) of San Gimignano.

Cenni, and was painted around 1413. The loggia next to the church was also frescoed by Cenni with a *Crucifixion*, totally painted by him, plus a series of other scenes most of which are greatly damaged; he moreover "restored" or repainted a larger, much older fresco depicting the *Madonna and Child in glory with angels*. The image was probably much venerated, as Cenni did not dare to repaint the Madonna's face, which is pure early 14th century, and reminds one of Simone Martini's style. If this great Sienese master painted the earlier work, we could be certain that he spent some time in San Gimignano, when Lippo, Federico Memmi and perhaps even his brother Donato Martini were there. Regarding the so-called Spezieria of the Hospital of St. Fina, the appurtenances of which are temporarily housed in this walled-up loggia (it was walled up in 1561, to serve as an oratory), see page 91.

Not far from the Castle, but outside the walls, we come across the lovely old *Springs* (Fonti) of San Gimignano. To reach them, one walks down the *Via delle Fonti*, after passing beneath the lonely, majestic *Porta alle Fonti* (Gate at the Springs) which

The noble Gateway of the Springs (Porta alle Fonti).

preserves all its hoary charm, and tread on downward along the narrow, beaten earth-track. The Springs are protected by ten stone arches: the four central ones are the oldest (12th century), the two larger ones on the right, also Romanesque, are 13th century, whilst the remaining four, with their great ogival arches, are 14th century Gothic.

On our way back towards Piazza della Cisterna, we take Via del Castello again and turn off to see the *House of St. Fina*, the meek Virgin Patron Saint of San Gimignano, who died in her girlhood on the 12th March 1253. Her name was Fina dei Ciardi. To reach her minute house, one turns down the narrow picturesque alley called Vicolo or Via Santa Fina, which is completely vaulted over in stone and brick, as if it were a tunnel. The saint's house is a modest medieval dwelling, dug into the hillside, consisting of two rooms and a sort of cave in the tufaceous rock where, according to legend St. Fina lay on the ground, on her wooden pallet, (now preserved on the altar of the Hospital Oratory).

Left: **the Becci and Cugnanesi Arch (Arco dei Becci e dei Cugnanesi)**; *right*: **the beginning of via San Giovanni.**

VIA SAN GIOVANNI

From Piazza della Cisterna, through the *Archway of the Becci and the Cugnanesi* (the two 13th century towers of which soar up to the right and to the left of the arch itself), one continues downhill along Via San Giovanni. The archway we have just walked beneath was in effect the Southern gate of the earliest walls of the town. *Via San Giovanni* is not only one of the most striking streets in the town, but also one of the best known, as it is the most customary route to take to reach the centre of the town. It is lined on either side with noble buildings of great architectural interest, some of them being shortened tower houses. N. 14, *Palazzo Pratellesi*, certainly deserves especial mention (it used to belong to the Gamucci family): the central part was built in the 14th century - it has a solid stone façade at ground level and a first floor façade in brick, pierced by lovely twin-mullioned windows, with the slender columns dividing the trilobed arches and pierced little rose windows

Via San Giovanni.

beneath the arch of each window, with bands of animal figures in low relief. It is on this floor that we find the *civic library* and the *historical archives*. See a fine fresco of the *Mystical Wedding of St. Catherine of Alexandria*, by Tamagni.

To the left of Via San Giovanni, one encounters the remains of the ex-monastery of the Franciscans, who took over the *Mansion of the Knights of Malta*, the only extant part of which is the delightful white travertine façade of the little erstwhile church with its five little blind arches supported by semi-columns, in the Pisan style of the 13th century.

Via San Giovanni ends at the Gate of St. John (*Porta San Giovanni*) which pierces the last circle of the town's defences and seals-in the ancient centre of the burg on this side. The door was constructed in 1262 and a few years later the so-

Above: the Gate of St. John (Porta San Giovanni) and the door of the ex-church of the "Madonna dei Lumi" (of the Lights); *below:* the façade of the ex-Franciscan monastery in via San Giovanni.

called "Castellaccia", used as a kind of guard-room by the night-watch was built above it. The *little bell-tower* on the left used to belong to the 17th century church known as the "Madonna of the Lights", demolished during the last century.

THIRD ITINERARY

From the Cathedral square along
Via San Matteo to Sant'Agostino —
San Pietro — San Jacopo dei Templari —
San Girolamo — Hospital of St. Fina

Left: the Arch of the Chancellory; *right:* Church of San Bartolo
and Palazzo Nomi Brogi Pesciolini in Via San Matteo.

The most important church in San Gimignano, after the
Cathedral of the Collegiata, is assuredly the church of
Sant'Agostino, which has such a wealth of works of art within
its walls that it could be considered a museum. From the
Cathedral square, one takes *Via San Matteo*, which together
with Via San Giovanni, splits the town in two and is as
splendid as the latter. At the beginning of the street, we
encounter the *Archway of the Chancellory* (Arco della Cancelleria), which used to be the Northern gate of the first circle

Left: **the Gate of St. Matthew (Porta San Matteo);** *right:* **via San Matteo.**

of the town-walls, just as the Arch of the Becci used to be the Southern gate. Almost immediately afterwards, on the right, we find the *Church of San Bartolo*, built entirely in brick and distinguished by two orders of little arches: five for each register, in accordance with the dictates of the 13th century Romanesque style. The cross of the Knights Templar is above the door lintel. A much restored Romanesque interior.

The massive russet bulk of the *Tower Mansion* which used to belong to the *Nomi Brogi Pesciolini* rises near the church: a typically 13th century building with four registers, pierced by elegant twin-mullioned windows, some of which have been walled-up or restored. The whole of Via San Matteo is a succession of strongly built 13th and 14th century edifices (although many of them have been considerably restored), with courtyards and loggias. *Palazzo Boldrini* (once of the Venerosi Pesciolini family) at No. 93, with frescoed 16th century grotesques and portraits of members of the Pesciolini family and landscapes.

Via San Matteo ends at the Gate of St. Matthew (*Porta San Matteo*). Just before actually going through the gate, one turns right, into *Via Cellolese* which leads into *Piazza Sant'Agostino*, where we are confronted by the Monastery and Church of Sant'Agostino.

The square of Sant'Agostino with the church of Sant'Agostino in the background.

SANT'AGOSTINO

The church is a typical monastic Gothic building (1298), entirely in brick, with tall, narrow Gothic windows piercing its sides. The interior is very wide, aisleless and covered by a beamed roof, whilst the choir and the transept side chapels are vaulted. The church contains priceless carved and painted masterpieces. Normally, one enters through the right side-door, but we shall describe the church as though we were entering it via the main door on the façade. Immediately to the right, upon entering, we find one of the finest examples of Florentine Renaissance art, designed and carved by Benedetto da Maiano, who, as we have already seen, was responsible for the altar and the decoration of the Chapel of St. Fina in the Collegiata Cathedral. His masterpiece in Sant'Agostino, is the splendid chapel of St. Bartolo, designed by Benedetto around 1495. The gleaming white altar shelters the sarcophagus containing the remains of the saint; on the lower register, beneath the urn, three episodes from his life: *the saint's toe, that fell-off into the hands of a priest who was washing his feet,*

Sant'Agostino · Interior.

miraculously re-attaches itself to the saint's foot; the death of St. Bartolo; a possessed woman is healed. Three, very elegant *Christian Virtues* sit in the three niches above the sarcophagus: *Faith, Charity and Hope.* Surrounded by a splendid garland, a *Madonna and Child,* adored by *two angels* crowns the whole. Sebastiano Mainardi frescoed the four *Doctors of the Church* against the vault of the chapel; he also frescoed *Sts. Gimignano, Lucy* and *Nicholas* on the left wall of the said chapel (c. 1500); the chapel floor is covered with majolica tiles (also early 1500s).

The right wall of the church: before we reach the side-door we mentioned above, we encounter the altar of St. Vincent, with a great altar-piece with predella, signed by Pier Francesco Fiorentino and dated 1494; it depicts a *Madonna and Child with Sts. Martin, Augustine, Stephen, Peter the Martyr, Bartholomew, Andrew, Vincent and Laurence.* At the feet of the Madonna, we find the diminutive figure of Friar Lorenzo di Bartolo, the sponsor. Higher up, in the lunette above the altar: a *Lamentation* and also a *St. Monica,* frescoed by Vincenzo Tamagni of San Gimignano, and much restored.

Beyond the side-door, there is a little frescoed *Lamentation over Christ,* with the Madonna, St. John and the symbols of the Passion; it is rightly attributed to Bartolo di Fredi (end of 14th century), the same master (more of whose work we shall

Left: the chapel of St. Bartolo; *right:* altar by Benedetto da Maiano; *below:* St. Gimignano, St. Lucy and St. Nicholas, by Sebastiano Mainardi (Sant'Agostino)

Madonna and Child with saints, by Pier Francesco Fiorentino
(Sant'Agostino).

admire in the first chapel of the transept) we have mentioned as the author of the great cycle of frescoes in the Collegiata. Other frescoes nearby, discovered in fragmentary form inside a great niche, depict the *Crucifixion* and, on the intrados of the arch: *St. Anthony Abbot*, a group with *St. Anne, the Madonna and Child, St. Augustine* and another *holy woman*, not easy to identify, because of the bad state of conservation of the fresco, have been attributed (R. Bartalini) to Biagio di Goro (late 14th-early 15th century). Continuing along the right side of the church we come to the first altar, upon which we find a painted terracotta statue of *St. Nicholas of Tolentino* (18th

Birth of the Virgin, by Bartolo di Fredi (Sant'Agostino).

century). The arched niche above the altar is frescoed with *Sts. Nicholas of Tolentino and Roch*; above: a *Madonna and Child with two angels*; on the intrados of the arch: *Sts. Onofrio and Paul the Hermit*. All the frescoes, dated 1529, are attributed to the workshop of Vincenzo Tamagni, whom we have already mentioned above. Faint traces of 14th century frescoes have come to light above the second altar (one can just detect a *Mary Magdalen*), which used to be covered by a 17th century canvas of the *Mystic Marriage of St. Catherine of Alexandria* (now in the last transept chapel). The first chapel of the right transept was completely frescoed by Bartolo di Fredi, probably during one of his lengthy stays in San Gimignano around 1374-'75. The frescoes illustrate episodes from the Life of the Madonna. The scenes that are still legible are the *Death of the Madonna*; the *bier* of the Assumption scene (the figure has disappeared); the *Birth of the Virgin*; *Presentation of the Virgin*

Left: **Coronation of the Virgin, by Piero del Pollaiolo;** *right:* **St. Augustine is accepted as a student at the University of Carthage** (detail), **by Benozzo Gozzoli** (Sant'Agostino).

at the Temple and the *Espousal to Joseph*. Upon the altar is the great alterpiece by Vincenzo Tamagni signed and dated 1523 which represents the *Birth of the Virgin*.

The main altar of the church of Sant'Agostino bears Piero del Pollaiolo's masterpiece (Piero was Antonio's brother and one of the greatest artists of the Renaissance). The great altarpiece depicts the *Coronation of the Virgin, surrounded by angels and Sts. Fina, Augustine, Bartolo, Gimignano, Jerome and Nicholas of Tolentino*. The painting was commissioned for this church by Friar Domenico Strambi and is signed and dated 1483: the elongated, rather angular forms somewhat attenuate the airy feeling of the composition and the Renaissance plasticity of the figures.

The choir contains the famous frescoes painted by another 15th century Florentine, whose work we have already admired in the Collegiata: the 17 episodes from the *Life of St. Augustine*, by Benozzo Gozzoli and painted between 1464 and '65 with the probable assistance of his helpers. This magnificent cycle covers all three walls of the choir (see the captioned plan), the vault (the *four Evangelists*), the intrados (*Jesus and the Apostles*) and the side-pillars of the altar (*St. Fina, the Archangel and Tobias, the Prophet Elijah, St. Nicolas of Bari, St. Nicholas of Tolentino and one of his miracles — St. Monica, St. Sebastian,*

Above: **St. Augustine leaves for Milan**; *below*: **St. Augustine lands at Ostia** (detail), **both by Benozzo Gozzoli** (Sant'Agostino).

St. Augustine teaches rhetoric at the University of Rome, by Benozzo Gozzoli (Sant'Agostino).

the martyrdom of the saint, St. John the Baptist, St. Gimignano, St. Bartolo and the Miracle of St. Bartolo's toe).

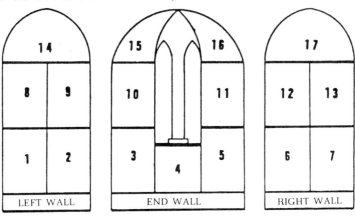

**St. Augustine entrusted to his grammar teacher, frescoed by
Benozzo Gozzoli** (Sant'Agostino).

1 — Augustine is entrusted by his parents, in Tagaste, to his
grammar teacher.

2 — He is admitted into the University of Carthage.

3 — Augustine's mother, St. Monica, blesses her son from
afar.

4 — Augustine sails to Italy (detached fresco, because of the
wall's bad state of conservation).

5 — He lands in Italy and is welcomed.

6 — Augustine teaches Rhetoric and Philosophy in Rome.

7 — He leaves Rome for Milan [the fresco bears the description of the commission granted to Benozzo Gozzoli by
Friar Domenico Strambi(«Doctor Parisinus») and the date
1465].

8 — Arrival of Augustine in Milan. He is received by St.
Ambrose and by the Emperor Theodosius.

9 — He attends the sermon of St. Ambrose, while his mother,
St. Monica begs the saint to convert her son. Augustine
discusses the Manichaean doctrine with St. Ambrose.

10 — He reads the Letters of St. Paul in front of his friend Alipius.

11 — The conversion of Augustine and his baptism by St. Ambrose in 464 (the fresco is dated April 1463).

12 — Jesus appears to Augustine on the sea-shore, as a Child to admonish the saint regarding the mystery of the Holy Trinity. St. Augustine explains the Rule of his Order to his friars. The saint visits the hermits on Mount Pisano.

13 — The death of St. Monica. In the background: St. Augustine sails back to Africa.

14 — Upon his consecration as a bishop, the saint blesses the citizens of Hippona.

15 — He confutes the heresy of Fortunatus.

16 — St. Augustine, in his study, in an exstatic trance, is told by St. Jerome about the joys of Heaven.

17 — The death of St. Augustine.

In the last chapel to the left of the transept, on the left wall: *Mystical marriage of St. Catherine of Alexandria* with a large number of other saints, dated 1589 and signed by the Florentine, Giovanni Balducci, known as "Il Cosci". On the right wall, is the canvas which used to cover the frescoes above the second altar on the right of the church, which we have just described: it depicts another *Mystical marriage of St. Catherine of Alexandria* and is to be attributed to an unknown 17th century Sienese artist.

Left wall: fresco of *St. Gimignano blessing three important personages of San Gimignano* (to wit: the poet Mattia Lupi, the canonical lawyer, Domenico Mainardi and the jurist, Nello Nelli de' Cetti. It was frescoed by Sebastiano Mainardi, who was commissioned to paint it in 1487 by Friar Domenico Strambi, known as "Doctor Parisinus" because he had taught at the University of Paris: his grave is beneath the fresco and has the frescoed recumbent figure of the monk himself above it. Also here, we find a marble low relief panel with *figures of bishops*: it is attributed to the great 14th century Sienese sculptor, Tino di Camaino, a follower of Giovanni Pisano. The panel probably belonged to the original sepulchre of St. Bartolo (c. 1318). Above the first altar we come to, one can distinguish traces of a great frescoed scene showing a *Madonna and Child between Sts. Michael and John the Baptist*. The work is important in mapping out Lippo Memmi's artistic career, as it was in all likelihood one of the earliest, if not Lippo Memmi's first work (probably painted together with his father Memmo di Filippuccio) before his Maestà in the Palace of the Commune of San Gimignano (1317). The *pulpit* is a Renaissance piece dated 1524 and is surmounted by a niche surrounding a frescoed *Crucifix* attributed to Tamagni.

Above: **St. Gimignano blessing three illustrious men, by Sebastiano Mainardi;** *below:* **Madonna and Child, angels and saints, by Fra Paolino da Pistoia** (Sant'Agostino).

St. Sebastian interceding for his people, by Benozzo Gozzoli;
pulpit and Crucifix attributed to Tamagni (Sant'Agostino).

Beneath it: two other monochrome sepia-coloured frescoed
Evangelists (or *Prophets*) also by Vincenzo Tamagni. Above the
second altar, a great fresco symbolizing *St. Sebastian interceding for his people*, showing the saint protecting the people of
San Gimignano beneath his cloak from the anger of the Lord:
a very spectacular work which is enlivened by the large
number of figures in the composition, although the helpers of
Benozzo Gozzoli, who was the main artist responsible for the
work — dated 28th July 1464 — occasionally reveal their
weaker hand. See also a marble bust of the "condottiero" (war-
band leader) *Niccolò Venerosi Pesciolini* (1618) by a Florentine
master whom R. Bartalini has identified as Pietro Tacca from
Carrara, a follower and pupil of Giambologna. The next niche
will contain the great altarpiece by Friar Paolino of Pistoia,
showing the *Madonna and Child with angels and saints* (1530).
On the wall, above: a fragmentary figure of a *saint*, 16th

Left: **Adoration of the Cross, by Vincenzo Tamagni**; *right*: **a view of the 15th century cloister** (Sant'Agostino).

century. Above the third altar, another fresco with the *Adoration of the Cross*, also by the 16th century San Gimignano master Vincenzo Tamagni. Against the inner façade: an altar with great canvas depicting the *Madonna of the Rosary* surrounded by a series of little oval canvases showing the *Misteries of the Rosary* (15th century - Unknown 17th century artist).

The Monastery of St. Augustine still possesses a lovely 15th century cloister with a loggia sustained by wide arches supported by slender columns.

SAN PIETRO

The church of San Pietro is on the piazza Sant'Agostino. It is Romanesque in style and is recorded as already in existence in a bull dated 1220. The outer walls are still plain brick and must have contrasted sharply with a once richly decorated interior. The early 14th century Sienese School frescoes that have been deciphered on its inner walls are in effect very beautiful, the most striking among them being the one depicting an erect Madonna holding her Son by the hand flanked by Sts. Paul

Left: **the church of San Pietro;** *right:* **the Madonna taking Her Child for a walk (Madonna del passeggio), attributed to the "Chompagno" of Simone Martini** (San Pietro).

and John the Baptist (*Our Lady a-walking* or Madonna del Passeggio); it could be attributed to a "chompagno" of Simone Martini, much akin to Lippo Memmi and to the so-called "Barna da Siena". Other important frescoes: a short cycle with an *Annunciation*, a *Madonna and Child enthroned* and a *Homage of the three Magi*, which are of fundamental importance in the study of the works of Memmo di Filippuccio; another fresco (14th century) of a *Madonna and Child enthroned flanked by two female saints*, unfortunately much deteriorated. Left of the altar: *Adoration of the Cross*: fresco by a master of the School of Duccio, akin to Niccolò di Segna (early 14th century). Above the main altar: a 16th century altarpiece showing a *Madonna and Child enthroned with saints*. On the left wall a fine painted wooden *Crucifix* (14th century) by a master revealing North European Gothic influences.

If the visitor can afford to spend a little extra time in San Gimignano, the following should not be missed:

CHURCH OF SAN JACOPO DEI TEMPLARI (next to the Hospital of St. Fina and the Springs) — a noble Romanesque edifice built at the beginning of the 13th century, with a parti-coloured facing in travertine and brick (the upper portion), a Pisan type portal and a delicate rose-window in pierced brick.

Church of San Jacopo dei Templari.

The church contains some admirable early 14th century frescoes attributable to Memmo di Filippuccio, that depict a *Madonna and Child enthroned with Sts. James and John*. The *Crucifixion* scene and the *Deposition from the Cross* both belong to the 14th century, as well.

CHURCH AND MONASTERY OF ST. JEROME. — Inside the church, above the main altar, an altarpiece with the *Madonna and Child enthroned with saints*, which can be defined as Vincenzo Tamagni's masterpiece; the altarpiece is signed and dated 1522. The Eternal Father in glory was added later on. On the left wall: another panel depicting the *Holy Family* and *St. John the Baptist* as a child, by a 16th century Florentine, akin to the group of artists who decorated Francesco Ist's "Studiolo" in Palazzo della Signoria in Florence (1570-'72); it particularly recalls the style of the "Northern" painter, Giovanni lo Stradano as well as reminding one of Jacopo Zucchi. Inside the monastery: interesting frescoes by a 16th century Florentine master.

HOSPITAL OF ST. FINA. — Founded in 1253 as the direct result of the surge of popular devotion immediately after the death of the San Gimignano saint. It is the only surviving hospital of the many little hospices in the medieval town and contains a number of important works of art.

In the entrance hall: two painted marble busts of *St. Fina and St. Gregory, Pope*: they are almost certainly by Pietro Torrigiani, known as "Il Torrigiano", Michelangelo's rival, who is famed for having given the great Florentine sculptor the punch on the nose that "marked" Michelangelo for life. The two busts, together with the other sculptures by Torrigiano, come from Rome, brought to San Gimignano by Canon Stefano Coppi, of San Gimignano and Rector of the Roman church of San Salvatore alla Suburra. The four frescoed busts of *Saints* surrounded by a circle are by Sebastiano Mainardi. In the little hall immediately after the vestibule: a decorative *frieze of cherubs or babies* which surround the *bust of St. Fina*, like a garland, attributed to Vincenzo Tamagni. In the Oratory of the Hospital, above the altar, there is the much venerated *wooden pallet* of St. Fina.

THE "SPEZIERIA" OR PHARMACY OF THE HOSPITAL OF ST. FINA.

— Because of their great interest, we must now describe what are known as the appurtenances of the Pharmacy of St. Fina which is situated near the ancient Hospital dedicated to the saint. The "Spezieria" or Pharmacy was begun in 1505 and existed for over three centuries and a half. What was left of its furnishings was bought by the Municipality of San Gimignano in 1906, piled up in a room and now, after being restored and studied by fascinated researchers, is temporarily exhibited in the church of San Lorenzo in Ponte. An exhibition — organized in 1981 (as well as the catalogue that illustrated it) — revealed the importance of this material as well as its scientific and art-historical aspects, as a large number of vases (some of which were still sealed and bore the indications on them revealing their contents) enabled the researchers to analyse medicinary substances of the most varied nature, thus allowing them to find out exactly which products were used for the healing of the sick in the hospital. The products ranged from well-known herb extracts or "simples" (some of which, however, were not always so easy to find from the "herbalists" studded around the countryside), to incredibly complex mixtures of substances that sound quite "unmedicinal" to our ears, such as ground precious stones (pearls, coral, amber, emeralds, garnets, aquamarines, ruby roots, etc.), ivory dust and minerals in general, chicken fat, crabs' eyes (calcite and aragonite), "dragon's blood", scorpion's oil, etc. as well as talismans and amulets of every description. The majolica vessels from the Spezieria are 228 and range from manufacts of the 15th to the 17th centuries, most of them

A number of vases from the Dispensary of the Hospital of St. Fina (now in the church of San Lorenzo in Ponte).

finely painted and enamelled. Their artistic value is very high and they offer an almost unique opportunity for an accurate study of the development of the potter's art in Tuscany and especially in the Val d'Elsa. The shapes of the vases are the characteristic forms used in pharmacies: jugs, jars, two-handled amphorae, mugs, etc.

There are also 92 extremely rare and interesting glass vessels, of unique value, due to the fragility of this material. The pieces date from the end of the 16th century (ampoules, little flasks and cylindrical jars) to the 18th century (jars, pots and bottles). They were indubitably produced locally.

SURROUNDINGS OF SAN GIMIGNANO

CELLOLE – The only trace of the ancient Burg of Cellole (or Cellore), which was feudally subject to the Cadolingi Counts of Fucecchio and rose near the site of an Etruscan necropolis, is the Romanesque Parish Church (Pieve) of Cellole that was built some time around 1190 and consecrated in 1237, as confirmed by the two original plaques. It is a lonely spot, now, surrounded by a grove of typically Tuscan cypresses.

The Pieve or church is entirely in stone, with an impressive façade pierced by a mullioned window divided by an elegant

18th century map of the "Community" of San Gimignano.

little column. The powerful, majestically built interior is the traditional Romanesque basilica type structure, with three aisles divided by massive columns and vaguely Pisan-looking pillars, rising to support rounded arches. A very interesting baptismal font hewn out of a single block for total immersion-type baptisms.

PANCOLE – Already mentioned in a document dated 6th April 1109, in which Ugo di Uguccione dei Cadolingi confirmed that the Abbot of Badia Morrona would have lordship over certain castles. The lovely church of Pancole was built in 1670, thanks to funds raised by the parishioners who wished to offer a worthy shrine to a frescoed image of the *Madonna*, attributed to Pier Francesco Fiorentino, they much venerated. The image had probably belonged to a rustic road-shrine, but the prodigious happenings that took place around it caused the larger building to be constructed, in what, in view of the year in

Left: the Parish Church of Cellole (Pieve di Cellole); *right:* detail of the interior.

which it was built, should have been in the Baroque style. Notwithstanding large-scale restructuring and restoration due to the precarious state of the building — seriously damaged during the IInd World War — we find ourselves, in effect, confronted by a most impressive late Florentine Renaissance-looking edifice, which has taken-in more than one expert. The architectural elements are thrown into high relief thanks to the presence of grey "pietra serena" pillars, pilasters, arches and friezes, that are given stately prominence by the white-washed walls. The spacious, echoing interior is crowned by a great octagonal dome.

CHURCH AND MONASTERY OF SANTA MARIA DI MON-TEOLIVETO – It rises amidst a very Tuscan landscape. One can still observe traces of the old monastery that was commissioned together with the church in 1340 by Gualtiero Salvucci and was subsequently enlarged in the 15th century. The church with its lovely brick bell-tower possesses a porch and still shelters a number of fine works of art, including a panel by Sebastiano Mainardi. The most important painting, however, is probably the great Benozzo Gozzoli (and workshop) fresco in the cloister of the Monastery, depicting a *Crucifixion with saints*. It is dated 1466.

© Copyright 1998 by Bonechi Edizioni "Il Turismo" S.r.l.
Via dei Rustici, 5 - 50122 FLORENCE
Tel. +39 (55) 239.82.24 - Fax +39 (55) 21.63.66
E-mail address: barbara@bonechi.com / bbonechi@dada.it
http://www.bonechi.com

Photos: Bonechi Edizioni "Il Turismo" S.r.l. Archives
Photos: Photographic archives of the Superintendency of the Artistic and Historical Assets for the Provinces of Siena and Grosseto; Foto Grassi, Siena; Arold Spindles; Studio M.B., Florence; Luciano Lazzari; Rolando Fusi.
Layout, cover and graphic design: Piero Bonechi and Rolando Fusi
Maps and graphics: Bonechi Edizioni "Il Turismo" S.r.l.
Project coordination and editing: Barbara Bonechi
Translation: Rosalynd Pio
Typesetting: Leadercomp, Florence
Reproductions: La Fotolitografia, Florence
Print: BO.BA.DO.MA., Florence
ISBN 88-7204-360-3